THE TURQUOISE BEE

The Turquoise Bee

THE LOVESONGS OF THE
SIXTH DALAI LAMA

Rick Fields
Brian Cutillo
Mayumi Oda

HarperSanFrancisco
A Division of HarperCollins*Publishers*

Tibetan calligraphy, Ume literary script, by Brian Cutillo.

THE TURQUOISE BEE: *The Lovesongs of the Sixth Dalai
Lama.* Copyright © 1998 by Rick Fields, Brian Cutillo,
Mayumi Oda. All rights reserved. Printed in the United
States of America. No part of this book may be used or
reproduced in any manner whatsoever without written
permission except in the case of brief quotations embod-
ied in critical articles and reviews. For information ad-
dress HarperCollins Publishers, 10 East 58rd Street, New
York, NY 10022.

FIRST EDITION

Library of Congress Cataloging-in-Publication Data

Fields, Rick.
   The turquoise bee : the lovesongs of the
   Sixth Dalai Lama / Rick Fields, Brian Cutillo,
   Mayumi Oda.—lst ed.
      p.   cm.
   Includes bibliographical references.
   ISBN 0–06–250810–8 (alk. paper)
   ISBN 0–06–250811–1 (pbk.)
   1. Tshans-dbyans-rgya-mtsho, Dalai Lama VI,
   1688-1706—Criticism and interpretation.
   I. Cutillo, Brian.   II. Oda, Mayumi.
   III. Title.
PL8748.T75Z66 1994   98-81478
895.41—dc20   CIP

94 95 96 97 98 ❖ RRD(H) 10 9 8 7 6 5 4 8 2 1

This edition is printed on acid-free paper that meets the
American National Standards Institute Z89.48 Standard.

To the Tibetan people
in their struggle for freedom.

Footsteps in the Snow

Face to face with a venerable lama
Having come to ask for spiritual guidance
My mind won't stay—
It slips away toward my lover.

THE SINGER of this and other lovesongs, Tsangyang Tshomo Gyatso—the Ocean of Melodious Song—was a man suspended between worlds. He was at once the Sixth Dalai Lama, the spiritual and secular head of Tibet, and also—in the words of L.C. Petech—"one of the finest poets of Tibet, nay, the only erotic poet of that country." He was the incarnation of Avalokitesvara, the Buddha of Compassion, and he was a young man with a well-developed taste for women, wine, and song. He was uninterested in the intricate political intrigues of eighteenth-century Tibet, and yet his role as a pawn in those same intrigues ultimately cost him his life. And finally, he was either a "false" Dalai Lama, who lived a corrupt and dissolute life, or an advanced Tantric yogi, who had mastered the secret path by which one could reach the bliss of the spirit by way of the joys of the flesh.

To the Tibetans, he was *both* Dalai Lama and lover, both spiritual teacher and poet. In his poem, he refers to himself as "The Turquoise Bee," a familiar conceit in Tibetan folk poems and songs.

Wandering minstrels sang his songs on the streets of Lhasa; young men sang them in the taverns; yakherders murmured them in the high mountain pastures. Everyone could sympathize with the bittersweet stories his songs recounted and with the unpretentious, vulnerable, and independent spirit they revealed. Here was a human being like all other human beings, who experienced the greatest heights and the lowest depths in one life; who fearlessly embraced both desire and truth; and who demonstrated how to live with compassion and awareness in the midst of a world driven by power, jealousy, and ignorance.

The Tibetans continue to revere the Sixth Dalai Lama to this day. "If anything, the stories [about the Sixth Dalai Lama] only serve to make him all the more popular and beloved," writes Thubten Jigme Norbu, brother of the present and Fourteenth Dalai Lama, "for it seems to us that to be born great and good makes great and good living and dying too easy. To be born otherwise, to grow as an ordinary man, with all the desires, the loves and hates, of ordinary man, then to *become* great and good, that is an achievement deserving of respect. It is also a lesson from which we can learn, for what can we learn from a man born otherwise than ourselves?"

ACCORDING TO the teachings of the Buddha, all sentient beings are (or have the innate capacity to become) buddhas—enlightened or, more precisely, "awakened ones."

Some of these fully evolved beings, however, are so moved by the suffering of the world that they become bodhisattvas, postponing their own entrance into the enlightened state to remain in the world, where they can help others dispel their ignorance and obtain liberation. Chief among these is Avalokitesvara, the Bodhisattva of Compassion, and the patron bodhisattva of Tibet.

The notion that bodhisattvas and other highly developed spiritual masters could take rebirth in human form was prevalent in India even before the time of the Buddha. But in Tibet, this doctrine was elaborated. A whole system of incarnated spiritual teachers and leaders developed. Sometimes these spiritual teachers left letters or poems indicating the time and place of their rebirth; sometimes the utterances of oracles possessed by a god led the way; sometimes a dream or vision pointed to the right child. In the case of the more important incarnations, like that of the Dalai Lama, there were tests to pass. Often, for example, the child was presented with an array of rosaries or bells, only one of which had belonged to him in his previous life. Only if he picked the right one without hesitation would he be considered.

The First Dalai Lama was Gechen Gyaldo, a leader of the New Translation reformed school—known as the Gelukpa, or Virtuous Ones—founded by Tsong Khapa in the fourteenth century. Like all Tibetan Buddhists, the Gelukpa were followers of the Tantric or Vajrayana, the "Diamond Vehicle" that had originated in India. According to this teaching, it was possible for a dedicated practitioner to attain liberation in one lifetime by making use of special practices. Most of these skillful means were purely meditative in character and involved the use of mantra, yogic exercises, and visualization.

Some of the oldest Tantric schools, however, also included certain secret disciplines involving a consort or yogic partner of the opposite sex. These enabled the practitioner to harness and transform sexuality, as well as other passions, as an aid on the path to enlightenment. The yogis and lamas of the oldest of these schools—the Nyingmapa, or Ancient Ones—were often married laymen. Some of them were highly accomplished practitioners of Dzogchen, or Great Perfection, meditation; others, however, seemed to have functioned as traveling magicians, fortune-tellers, and exorcists, who misused the Tantric teachings as an excuse to indulge in worldly pleasures.

Partly in reaction to this degeneration, whether real or imaginary, the Gelukpa emphasized a disciplined monastic life, including strict celibacy and a systematic study of Buddhist philosophy and logic, as well as a graded step-by-step course of meditation. Advanced Tantric practices were included in the Gelukpa curriculum, but were taught to followers only after they had participated in a long period of study. The sexual symbolism of the old Tantras remained as an inner meditation rather than an actual rite.

The Gelukpas rose to political power when the Third Dalai Lama converted the leader of the Altan Mongols, who installed him as the ruler of Tibet. His leadership was opposed, however, by a coalition of followers of the old translation schools and Tibetan nobles. By the time of the Fifth Dalai Lama, the country had fallen into a state of near anarchy.

The Great Fifth Dalai Lama, as he came to be known, was a prolific scholar, who left works on philosophy, history, and poetics. He was also a deeply compelling spiritual leader. His meeting with Gushri Khan in 1638 resulted in the conversion of the Khan and all his tribesmen to the Gelukpa doctrine. With the Khan backing him, he succeeded in uniting the warring factions of Tibet and ushered in a period of peace. He also visited the Manchu emperor, Shun-chi, at his court in Peking, cultivating cordial relations with the emperor, who was himself an ardent Buddhist. In 1645, he moved his government to Lhasa and laid the foundation for his fortified palace, the Potala, on Red Hill, amidst the ruins of the palace of the king who had brought Buddhism to Tibet in the eighth century. Like the Dalai Lamas, this king was considered an incarnation of Avalokitesvara, and the hill had long been thought to be the sacred abode of the bodhisattva.

During the long reign of the Great Fifth, sectarian rivalry diminished—or at least became less violent. In fact, though he by no means neglected the monks and scholars of his own Gelukpa school, the Great Fifth exhibited a rather unorthodox predilection for the old Tantric school of the Nyingmapa. One of his closest teachers was a master of the Dzogchen, or Great Perfection, teachings of the Nyingmapa.

During the last three years of his life, the Fifth Dalai Lama withdrew from public life, devoting himself more intensively to his spiritual life. He entrusted his affairs to the Desi—his regent or chief minister—who had been groomed for this position since childhood, first by his uncle, who was the former Desi, and then by the Great Fifth himself. Indeed, it was commonly thought that the Desi was actually the Great Fifth's son. This idea was partly given currency by the Great Fifth's Nyingma leanings. It was also fueled by a popular song recounting how the Great Fifth's rosary had been found in the house where the Desi was born. None of the rumors, however, affected the high esteem in which the Great Fifth was held.

The Desi—who was destined to play a key role in the life of the Sixth Dalai Lama—was an immensely gifted and worldly man. An erudite scholar, he was the author of treatises on history, medicine, rhetoric, and astrology. At the same time, he had a taste for the sensual things in life. He was celebrated for his skill on the *piwang,* the Tibetan lute. He was also known to have had numerous affairs, and it was whispered that no attractive woman—or young boy—was safe from his advances.

Everyone agreed that he was a dedicated and able administrator. He personally visited all the various courts and departments that fell under his jurisdiction. Sometimes he would disguise himself and go out among the people to find out what they were thinking. One famous story tells how he asked a grizzled guard-monk what he thought of the Desi's administration. "Politics is for the Desi," the monk replied. "As for me, all I care about is drinking the *chang* hidden under my bed."

When the Great Fifth died in 1682, the Desi kept his death a secret. He let it be known that the Great Fifth had entered a strict meditation retreat and could not be disturbed, and he went to extraordinary lengths to prevent anyone from discovering the truth. Food and drink were prepared for the Great Fifth and left outside his chambers every day. Occasionally, the sound of the Great Fifth's tantric bell and drum could be heard. When state papers needed to be signed, the Desi would disappear into the Dalai Lama's private sanctum and reappear with the papers stamped with the Dalai Lama's personal seal.

Sometimes the Desi made use of a monk who bore a resemblance to the Great Fifth. The impostor received a Mongolian delegation wearing an eye-shade, because his eyes were not large and round like the Great Fifth's, and a hat, because his head was not completely bald like the Great Fifth's. This and other occasional sightings of the Great Fifth served to dispel any rumors about his death.

In addition to the impostor, who had to be threatened and bribed to keep up the charade, a few other members of the Desi's inner circle were aware of the secret. But when the state oracle, whom the Desi had consulted about affairs of state, seemed to have become aware of the Desi's ploy, the Desi took no chances. The oracle, as well as his sister, was put to death.

It might appear that the Desi was keeping the Great Fifth's demise secret purely for his own purposes. But that does not seem to be the case—or at least not the whole case. The Desi did send out clandestine search parties, made up of a few trusted ministers, to seek out the Great Fifth's reincarnation shortly after his death. Sure enough, in 1685, the discovery of an extraordinary young boy was reported in the border district of Mon. His family were adherents of the Nyingma and relatives of the great *terton*—or treasure-finder of hidden teachings—Jigme Lingpa of Bhutan.

These circumstance were not in themselves unusual. Incarnations of one school were often reborn in families belonging to another school. And it could even be argued that the new incarnation's Nyingma background was merely another indication of his authenticity, considering the Great Fifth's interests in the school.

His age *was* unusual. Incarnations were generally identified at an early age—by one or two. They often began their monastic training at the age of four or five, a practice which was thought to protect them from developing a taste for worldly pleasures. But the difficulties caused by the Desi's concealment meant that the Great Fifth's incarnation did not begin serious training until he was twelve. It is commonly thought that this "late start" was at least partly responsible for the Sixth Dalai Lama's unconventional life-style. We can probably assume that he had already developed the independent spirit which would stand him in such good stead—and get him into so much trouble—later in his life.

The young incarnation's situation was difficult from the very beginning. The Desi had ordered him brought under cover to a house in Tsona. But the local officials, who were naturally not informed of the real reasons for all the unusual security precautions, seem to have assumed the worst and treated the party more like prisoners than honored guests.

In 1697, when the Sixth Dalai Lama was fourteen, he and his family were moved to Nakartse, once again under the strictest security. This time, they were received as guests in the mansion of an uncle of the Great Fifth. The Panchen Lama, who had served as the Great Fifth's tutor, gave the Sixth Dalai Lama both the vows of a novice monk and a prophetic religious name—Tsanayang Gyatso, meaning Ocean of Melodious Song. Now the Desi felt he could reveal his secret. Ministers were sent out with the news that the Fifth Dalai Lama had died fifteen years earlier and that his new incarnation was on his way to Lhasa. A delegation also set forth to carry the same message to K'ang Hsi, the Manchu emperor in Peking.

The young boy now had an entourage befitting his new status. In addition to the Desi, he had gained a secretary, a chamberlain, attendants, and a tutor. The whole retinue made their way to Lhasa, stopping in the town of Nyethang. Here they were met by a large party of monks and state officials who made offerings to the new Dalai Lama before a great crowd. The Desi explained that the Great Fifth himself had instructed him to keep his death secret. According to the Desi, the Great Fifth had been concerned that if his death had become known to the various Mongol tribes, who had been held in check by their devotion to him, they would resume their wars, and work on the Potala would not be completed. What the Desi did not say, but what everyone probably knew very well, was that warfare among the Mongols could open the way for the Manchu emperor of China to conquer or, at least, control Tibet.

There is a story that the Desi had beseeched the dying Great Fifth to make the office of the Dalai Lama hereditary in order to avoid the dangerous interregnum between rulers. The Great Fifth supposedly agreed, and ordered that his successor be permitted the freedom to live as a layman. It was also said that the girl from Chung Gyal, referred to in one of the poems, was destined to be the mother of the Seventh Dalai Lama. This would have made the office of Dalai Lama hereditary. It was thought, according to the Tibetan historian Kalsung Dhondup, "Tibet would have become invincible to any foreign power. But it is believed that due to the general deterioration of Tibet's collective virtue, Tsangyang Gyatso never met the girl from Chung Gyel."[1]

Most Tibetans seem to have accepted the Desi's explanation. According to him, an old woman from Lhasa thanked him with the words, "For all these years the lord regent has alone carried the burden for the humans of this world while the Omniscient Conqueror [the Great Fifth] was not alive. And he has overseen all matters to do with the religious and secular spheres. Not realizing there was darkness, we saw the sun shining!"[2]

A few senior officials grumbled that he had concealed the Great Fifth's death far too long. Some of the Mongol princes were also angry at the Desi for his concealment.

But the most annoyed of all was K'ang Hsi, the Manchu emperor, who issued an edict to the Tibetan envoy: "If the Dalai Lama is dead, in principle, it is right to inform all the Lords-Protectors of the Faith. . . . We repeatedly sent envoys to ask him. The Desi did not let any of the envoys have an interview with the Dalai Lama. Falsely, he told them that the Dalai Lama was living on the top of

11

a high tower." The edict ended on an ominous note: "The Desi," charged the emperor, "is deceiving the Dalai Lama and the Panchen Lama, and is destroying the faith of Tsong Khapa."[3]

For the moment, the Desi's audacious ruse seemed to have worked. The Sixth Dalai Lama proceeded to Lhasa and took up residence in the Potala. His formal enthronement that winter was witnessed by state officials, monks from the three major monasteries, Mongol princes, and representatives of the Manchu emperor.

The Sixth Dalai Lama's training now began in earnest, and he applied himself with great intelligence to his spiritual and secular studies. It soon became clear to his teachers that this Dalai Lama was different from all other Dalai Lamas. He appeared to have no interest in monastic discipline. Neither did he seem to have any taste for the ceremony and protocol that played such an important role in the life of a Dalai Lama. Instead, he lived simply and unostentatiously. In the Potala, he did without servants and courtiers, brewing his own tea and serving his own guests.

Outside the Potala, he went on foot instead of riding horseback. He spent most of his days practicing archery and going on picnics with his aristocratic young friends. When he delivered the religious discourses that were part of his training, he bypassed the learned monks in the assembly halls and spoke instead to ordinary people in the public parks in language they could understand.

But now *he* had a secret. During the day, as we know from his poems, he had to conceal the affairs he had with the ladies of the aristocracy. His love poems from this period tell of flirtations with daughters of great officials, of catching a smile from his seat in the row of lamas, and of the ever-present need for secrecy.

At night, he would rise from his chambers in the upper palace, don a disguise, and surreptitiously slip out a backdoor. He would make his way across the fields to Shol-town, a disreputable section of lower Lhasa. There he would carouse in taverns and brothels, drinking *chang* (the powerful milky-white Tibetan barley beer), singing songs, gambling, and often spending the night with whichever lady had stolen his heart. Judging by his poems, he experienced both the ecstasies and anguish of any romantic youth.

Before the sun rose, he would retrace his steps, quietly open the backdoor, tiptoe through the ornate halls and waiting rooms of the Potala, and slip into bed. When morning came, he would commence his duties as the Dalai Lama.

For a while, he was able to conceal his nightly jaunts. But one morning—the story is related in one of his most famous poems—an attendant noticed footprints in the snow leading to the back door of the Potala. He followed them to a tavern in Shol-town. The Sixth Dalai Lama was exposed.

The Desi had continued to pressure the young man to take the full monastic ordination from the

Panchen Lama, but Tsangyang Gyatso had so far managed to avoid the issue. Finally, the Desi asked the Panchen Lama to come to Lhasa to convince the Dalai Lama himself. The Sixth Dalai Lama apparently learned of the Desi's plans and announced that he had decided to journey to the Panchen Lama's monastery, Tashi Lhunpo, to receive the vows.

The Panchen Lama came to meet him and escort him back. But instead of going to Tashi Lhunpo, the Sixth Dalai Lama made a detour to the town of Shigatse. When he finally arrived for the ordination ceremony, an imposing crowd of dignitaries were waiting. Tsangyang Gyatso surprised them again. He prostrated three times before the Panchen Lama, first reciting, "I confess to breaking my lama's commands," and then announcing, in front of all the assembled guests, that he would not receive the full monastic vows. Even worse, he insisted on giving up his novice vows as well.

The lamas and nobles pleaded, cajoled, coaxed, and appealed to his sense of duty, but the Dalai Lama held his ground. Finally, it is said, the young Dalai Lama threatened to put an end to his own life if the issue were forced. Faced with this ultimatum, the lamas and nobles had no choice but to accede.

The Sixth Dalai Lama returned to Lhasa his own man. He was no longer a monk, but he was still the Dalai Lama. There was no rule that said the Dalai Lama had to be a monk, though he always had been and, it was assumed, always would be. Nor, for that matter, was there a rule dictating the shape or form an incarnation of Avalokitesvara must take. In fact, there were numerous stories about bodhisattvas who had appeared in whatever form was most helpful at the time, including tavern girls and dissolute youths.

The Dalai Lama was now able to live openly as a layman. He dressed in light blue silk brocades, let his hair grow long, and decorated his fingers with elegant rings. He went about carrying his beloved bow and quiver and practiced archery at the back of the Potala with his young friends. He wandered around the country side "according to his will." And he continued to visit his old haunts in Shol-town, some of which were painted yellow in commemoration of the nights the Dalai Lama spent there with his lovers.

A contemporary account by Lelung Jedrung Lobsang Trinley, translated by Michael Aris in his *Hidden Treasures and Secret Lives,* reports an encounter with Tsangyang Gyatso in a house in a small village. The Sixth Dalai Lama was accompanied by his attendants and a few officials, all of whom were so drunk "they could not stand up but leaned against each other in a complete stupor." The Sixth Dalai Lama, however, "gave counsels, wrote compositions, and sang songs without error, being not in the least altered [by the effect of alcohol]." [4]

In the Potala, the Sixth Dalai Lama proved himself a gifted architect. The mortar and cement that held together the towering walls of the Potala had been dug from a clay quarry that now gaped unattractively behind the Red Hill. Tsangyang Gyatso had the quarry flooded to create a large pool. He named the pool after the Naga, the water-spirit serpent who, with his seven hoods, had shielded the Buddha from a great thunderstorm after his enlightenment. He then had built the lovely Naga temple, which he had designed as a Chinese pavilion. The pavilion gave him a place to entertain his friends and meet his lovers outside the sacrosanct precincts of the Potala.

Tsangyang Gyatso's carefree ways put the Desi in a difficult position. On the one hand, he cautioned people against criticizing the Dalai Lama, who was, after all, the incarnation of Avalokitesvara and therefore the foundation of the Desi's power. On the other hand, people were talking more and more about the Sixth Dalai Lama's scandalous behavior. The Mongols in particular, who tended to be rather fundamentalist and puritanical Gelukpas, were beginning to voice their doubts.

The Desi took a desperate step. He decided that the Dalai Lama was being led astray by one of his friends, a young nobleman. As the Dalai Lama and his friend returned from archery practice one evening, they were attacked. The assailants intended to harm the Dalai Lama's friend, but they got his servant instead. The Dalai Lama had been in a playful mood that afternoon, and he had had the servant and master exchange their clothes.

The servant was killed in the attack while wearing his master's clothes.

The next morning, an enraged Dalai Lama consulted the oracle and the assailants were duly identified. One was paraded through the streets of Lhasa on a red-hot metal copper horse. The others were simply executed. The Desi managed to keep his part in the affair quiet, but the Dalai Lama was convinced he had instigated the attack. Relations between the Desi and his former protégé, already strained, now deteriorated completely.

Outside the Potala, both the Desi and the Sixth Dalai Lama faced more serious problems. The Qosot Mongol chieftain, Lozang Khan, hoping to assert his position as king—the position once enjoyed by his grandfather, Gushri Khan—had found a powerful ally in the Manchu emperor, K'ang Hsi. The Desi, meanwhile, had entered into friendly negotiations with another Mongol tribe, the Dzungars, with whom the Manchus were hostile. The Desi's possible alliance with the Dzungars was especially alarming to the Manchus. If the Dzungars gained the Dalai Lama's support, they might be able to once again unite the other Mongol tribes against the Manchu empire.

The Desi relied on intrigue once again. First he tried to poison Lozang Khan. When that failed, he attempted to assassinate him during the Great Prayer Festival of 1705. Lozang Khan responded by mounting a full-scale attack against the Desi, who was defeated in battle and then beheaded.

The Manchu emperor congratulated the Khan on a job well done, and sent imperial representatives "to support Lhazan Khan against the disaffected and to finish putting order among the Lama partisans of the Desi."

With the Desi out of the way, Lozang Khan and K'ang Hsi now turned their attention to the Sixth Dalai Lama. Lozang Khan accused the Sixth Dalai Lama of being not merely a dissolute and licentious youth, but a heretic who adhered to the dangerous teachings of his relative, the Nyingma treasure-finder Jigme Lingpa. These tantric teachings, which were always open to sensationalistic distortions, were painted in the most literal and lurid light. Lozang Khan reported to the emperor, for example, that members of the Sixth Dalai Lama's secret tantric circle "took women," and were "taught the offerings of the symbols of the private parts of men and women. . . . "[5]

K'ang Hsi may or may not have taken these charges seriously, but he decided that the time had come to depose the Sixth Dalai Lama. He nevertheless advanced with caution, reminding his councillors, "Although he is false, he still has the name Dalai Lama and all the Mongols follow him."

In Lhasa, Lozang Khan tried to prepare by putting the question of the Dalai Lama's fitness to a council of influential lamas and noblemen. But he did not find the unequivocal support he was looking for. The council concluded that "although they were shocked at his behavior,

Tsangyang Gyatso was the rightful Dalai Lama." They did add, however, that "the spiritual enlightenment (*bodhi*) no longer dwelt in him."[6]

Neither Lozang Khan nor anyone else could be certain what the learned lamas meant by that statement, but the Khan decided that he could wait no longer. On June 11, 1706, his troops removed the Sixth Dalai Lama from the Potala and brought him to the Lhaku gardens on the outskirts of Lhasa. When monks from the three great monasteries attempted to see him, they were forcefully driven back by the Khan's troops.

On June 27, Lozang Khan declared that Tsangyang Gyatso, the Sixth Dalai Lama, had been deposed and was summoned by imperial decree to go to Peking. As the party escorting the Dalai Lama moved out, a furious crowd of monks attacked them with sticks and stones. They succeeded in rescuing the Dalai Lama, who sought refuge in his summer residence, the Gaden palace at Drepung.

The next day, the monks hastily called for the state oracle. Possessed by the god, the oracle "proclaimed that whoever denied that Tsangyang Gyatso was the incarnation of the Great Fifth, was snared by devilish illusions." The jubilant monks vowed to defend the Dalai Lama at any cost.

On June 29, Lozang Khan's troops fired on the monastery with artillery. Realizing that the end was near, Tsangyang Gyatso turned to poetry one last time, composing one of his most famous and, at the time, enigmatic songs: "White crane, lend me your skill of wing," which was later considered a prophecy of his rebirth. He sent the poem to an unknown lady in Shol-town. Then, hoping to avoid a massacre, he walked out of the palace accompanied by two or three companions. As he was surrounded, he declared, "It's no matter if I live or die. I'll meet my lamas and monks again soon."[7] His companions went down fighting, and the Sixth Dalai Lama let himself be taken.

"He clearly acted with a greater love for others than for himself," a biographer of the Seventh Dalai Lama would write later. "Also, on the route, while cultivating 'the mind of enlightenment,' he read and pondered a great deal on the precepts which speak of how to turn evil circumstances to profit on the path to liberation, and he put them into practice."[8] Tsangyang Gyatso died near Kunganor Lake on the journey to Peking, on November 14, 1706, after writing a final death-poem in which he lamented, "things didn't go right in this life."

Official Chinese and Tibetan accounts say that he fell ill. Other accounts say he was executed or murdered. The Manchu Court was notified and they replied with terse instructions: "The false Dalai Lama, who had been sent under escort by Ha-Zan, came to fall ill outside the pass of Hsining, and died there of disease. The false Dalai Lama's behavior was perverse and disorderly. Since he has now died on the way, of disease, we ought to abandon the corpse. The Emperor approves of this proposal."[9]

Thus ended the life of the Sixth Dalai Lama. According to one source his body was cremated, the smoke drifting toward the city of Litang, before the emperor's order to abandon the body was received. Of all the Dalai Lamas, he is the only one whose remains are not enshrined in the Potala.

Lozang Khan installed his own Sixth Dalai Lama shortly after Tsangyang Gyatso's death. The new Sixth Dalai Lama was a young monk rumored to be the son of Lozang Khan. But even though he was enthroned with all the proper ceremonies, no one took the Khan's puppet seriously.

Lozang Khan's position was further undermined by reports from eastern Tibet that the Seventh Dalai Lama had been discovered in Litang. It was now realized that this was just what the Sixth Dalai Lama had prophesied in his last poem. There was a groundswell of support for the Litang Dalai Lama among the Tibetans, and many of the Mongol princes who journeyed to Litang to see the boy themselves came away ardent supporters. Officially, the Manchu emperor continued to back Lozang Khan and his Sixth Dalai Lama, but he thought it prudent to hedge his bets. Aware of the growing sentiment in favor of the Litang Dalai Lama, the emperor adopted a wait-and-see attitude, and managed to place the Litang boy in a kind of protective custody in the Kumbum monastery.

The Dzungars, too, were watching the boy. Claiming that they wanted only to restore the true

Dalai Lama—the Litang Dalai Lama—to the Tibetans, the Dzungars dispatched a raiding party to Kumbum. Meanwhile, their main forces moved toward Lhasa.

The raid to capture—or free—the Litang Dalai Lama did not succeed. But the Dzungars had come too far to go back. Aided by Tibetan sympathizers, who still believed that the Dzungars were bringing the Litang Dalai Lama with them, they stormed Lhasa. A bloody three-day sack ensued in which the tomb of the Fifth Dalai Lama was looted. Lozang Khan was hunted down and swiftly dispatched. The Dzungar reign of terror continued in Lhasa and beyond. A report from a party of Capuchin missionaries stationed in Lhasa stated that "during the whole of 1718 the Dzungars did nothing but practice unheard-of atrocities on the people of the kingdom."

The emperor's huge Manchu army entered Tibet in 1719. After consulting with various Mongol princes, he decided to support the Litang Dalai Lama. Official recognition came in the form of a great seal composed of gold and jewels and weighing 130 ounces that bore the words "Seal of the Sixth Dalai-Lama. Leader of the creatures, diffuser of the teachings" in Manchu, Mongolian, and Tibetan. As far as the Manchus were concerned, the inscription made clear that neither Tsangyang Gyatso nor the puppet installed by Lozang Khan had been the real Sixth Dalai Lama: that both of them had been accepted by the

Manchu emperor was conveniently overlooked. Lozang Khan's puppet Dalai Lama was quietly removed and retired to Peking.

The Litang Dalai Lama arrived in Lhasa along with the Manchu army. He was escorted into the ruined but still grand halls of the Potala by a procession of Mongol chiefs, Manchu officers, and Tibetan lamas and noblemen. Soon, the Panchen Lama arrived and gave the new Dalai Lama the vows of a novice monk. The Chinese still insisted that he was the Sixth Dalai Lama, but the Tibetans and the Mongols and the new Dalai Lama himself knew better. His predecessor, Tsangyang Gyatso, had been the Sixth Dalai Lama, and he was the Seventh.

WITH HIS mortal life ended and his spiritual lineage safely passed on, Tsangyang Gyatso entered the world of legend.

It was said that he had not really died at Kunganor Lake but had simply vanished in a great fog. According to one story, he had gone to live as a mountain yogi and sheepherder. According to another, he had reappeared as a beggar in Lhasa and had even been spotted in a crowd at the court of the Seventh Dalai Lama. But as soon as he had been recognized, he had vanished. Still another account, given in a text titled *The Secret Life of the Sixth Dalai Lama,* tells how he went on a pilgrimage to India and then spent forty years in missionary work among the Mongols.

Some Tibetans ascribe these multiple lives to yogic powers. The Thirteenth Dalai Lama, for example, accepted the possibility, but criticized it nonetheless. In a conversation recorded by the British diplomat Sir Charles Bell, he said that the Sixth Dalai Lama "did not observe even the rules of a fully ordained priest. He drank wine habitually. And he used to have his body in several places at the same time—in Lhasa, in Kongpo, and elsewhere. Even the place whence he retired to the Honorable Field is uncertain; one tomb of his is in Alashar in Mongolia, while there is another in the Rice Heap monastery. Showing many bodies at the same time is disallowed in all sects of our religion because it causes confusion in the work." The Thirteenth Dalai Lama went on, "One of his [the Sixth Dalai Lama's] bodies used to appear in the reception hall of the Seventh Dalai Lama. One is said to appear also at my reception, but I am unable to say whether this is true or not."[10]

What is true for us today, however, is that the Sixth Dalai Lama lives still another life. This is the life of his poems. We can hear him whispering sweet words in our ears, taking up his lute in taverns, drunk on *chang* and Dharma, musing on his strange fate, puncturing the pretensions of both worldly and spiritual braggarts, and, finally, singing an ecstatic vajrasong that joins bliss and emptiness.

His poems, like his life, remain controversial. At first sight, they seem to be simple folk-poems.

They are plain and unadorned, without much recourse to literary artifice. But as we look closer, the poems split open to reveal hidden depths.

In fact, most Tibetan commentators find that numerous songs contain hidden Tantric teachings. On the other hand, Mark Tatz, a scholar and translator of the songs, suggests in *The Tibet Journal* that the song most often cited as Tantric may be the result of an interpolation. "In any case," Tatz argues, "to rationalize his deeds in this way cuts the tension that is the very life of the songs."

We can also locate Tsangyang Gyatso within a Tibetan poetic lineage that combined the Tantric *dohas*—songs of Indian *siddhas* or yogis such as Saraha—with popular Tibetan folk songs that satirized the powerful and pompous. R. A. Stein characterizes this poetic tradition: "In early Tibet there were religious specialists, akin to bards, who expressed themselves in enigmatic poems or songs. . . . It happens that the religious circles which inherited this taste for songs and allegories, and developed them, also played an important part in drawing attention to the defects inherent in Tibetan society. These are impecunious wandering yogins characterized by unorthodox behavior. In Tibetan they are known as 'madmen' (*smyon-pa*), a word implying both eccentricity and 'divine' inspiration. They are fond of laughing and joking. They mix with the people and take their part. So they violently criticize the abuses of society, including the 'Church' and all the religious orders."[11]

25

When we see Tsangyang Gyatso in the light of this tradition, we can perhaps gain a deeper appreciation of his poetry. Most of these bards sang their songs from the margins of Tibetan society. But Tsangyang Gyatso sang from the very center of Tibetan political and ecclesiastical power. His poems, like his life, thus possess both an unusual authority and an unusual degree of ambivalence, irony, and paradox.

The poems express the inner life of a truly complex and enigmatic figure. He is the Dalai Lama, yet he also bares his heart as the blissful or unhappy lover. And he is torn between the renunciation of spiritual life and the passionate attachment of the lover's life.

Yet in another song, he is also a Tantric adept singing to the dakini (or goddess) of wisdom, transcending the conventional distinction between the secular and the spiritual. For the Tibetans, it is *this* Sixth Dalai Lama who is the key to both the life and songs. "To anyone who knows Tibet," as Thubten Jigme Norbu writes, "there is something at work here that is a great deal more than the mere love of a man for a woman, something that is much more consistent with the simplicity of life led by the Gyalwa Rinpoche [the Sixth Dalai Lama] in the Potala. It seems most possible that the young Tsangyang was initiated into tantric practices which involve physical, rather than mental, sexual intercourse with women." He goes on to point out: "There is no doubt that the young Tsangyang had all the physical urges of any youth when he entered monastic life. We can also be sure that his instructors, headed by his tutor, the Panchen Rinpoche, will have done everything in their power to lead him away from purely physical pleasures, and for this reason it is even more likely that he may have been initiated into tantric practices that would divert his physical desires into spiritual channels."

This may well be, but who knows? As with any true poet, the ongoing revelation of the mystery that is Tsangyang Gyatso's life can only be found in the heart-to-heart, mind-to-mind genius of the poems. They speak and sing for themselves. And in doing so they bring us what Thubten Jigme Norbu calls "Tsangyang Gyatso's most fundamental teaching, namely that life itself, in whatever form it appears to us, is one of our greatest teachers."

A Note on the Translation

There is no definitive edition of the songs of the Sixth Dalai Lama. The Sixth Dalai Lama's personal diary, which may have contained the complete poems, is either lost or not yet revealed. We have been liberal, perhaps even radical, in including every song we came across that has been attributed to Tsangyang Gyatso. Our compilation includes sixty-seven poems. There may be a few that Tsangyang Gyatso didn't actually sing or write himself, but there are none that he wouldn't have or couldn't have.

Most of the songs follow a traditional Tibetan folk song form. Most verses are in four lines of six syllables each. This is the measure traditionally used for secular songs. (Religious poetry uses lines of seven syllables.)

The lines tend to fall into parallel couplets. The first couplet often presents a figure drawn from ordinary life; the second uses this to make a point or draw a lesson. This is a common poetic teaching device in Buddhism as well as in other traditions.

We have tried to follow the original Tibetan as closely as possible. Elaborations and interpretations have been kept to a minimum. At the same time, we have followed the example of Tsangyang Gyatso and trusted our instincts. Because Tibetan is built by combining single-syllable words, we have preferred Anglo-Saxonisms to Latinisms. Because the Sixth Dalai Lama wrote in a robust, idiomatic language, we have reached for equivalents in contemporary American speech.

We have taken our greatest liberties with the order of the songs, but all compilations, including ours, begin with the same song. Most, including ours, end with the poem we have called "Song of Rebirth," though some include songs after that that were not likely composed by the Sixth Dalai Lama. We have departed from the traditional practice by grouping the songs according to subject matter and narrative. Notes on individual songs are included at the back of the book.

RICK FIELDS

Song of Setting Out

1

From East Hill peak,
The moon rose clear and white
Face not born of mother
Circles round and round in mind.

ཤར་ཕྱོགས་རི་བོའི་རྩེ་ནས།།
དཀར་གསལ་ཟླ་བ་ཤར་བྱུང་།།
 མ་སྐྱེས་ཨ་མའི་ཞལ་རས།།
ཡིད་ལ་འཁོར་འཁོར་བྱས་བྱུང་།།

Songs of Lhasa

2

Peacocks from the east of India!
Parrots from the valley of Kong!
Though born in different lands
All meet in Lhasa, Wheel of Dharma.

3

Like a bee caught in a web—
The thoughts of this young kid from Kongpo;
He's been my roommate for three days,
And is thinking of Dharma and his future.

4

In Lhasa the crowd is teeming.
But in Chung Gyal the girls are charming;
The lover I've been waiting for—
She's coming from Chung Gyal Valley.

5

What luck! The wind-horse leaps up,
A banner of fortune unfurled!
I'm invited to a great feast
For this noble family's daughter!

Songs of a Young Lover

6

Double hollyhock flowers—
If you are offered to the temple
Take me, the young turquoise bee,
With you
To the temple too.

7

Daughter of a great official—
Like seeing a ripe fruit,
The fine apricot of Kham
At the tip of the highest tree.

8

That girl who's stolen my mind—
If we could be together forever—
Like the joy of finding a jewel
Deep in the depths of the sea.

9

Lover met by chance on the road,
Girl with delicious-smelling body—
Like picking up a small white turquoise
Only to toss it away again.

10

White teeth smiling.
Brightness of skin.
On my seat in the high lama's row
At the quick edge of my glance
I caught her looking at me.

11

When the cuckoo arrives from Mon
The earth's spring essence wells up.
Since I met my lover
Body and mind have become relaxed.

12

The arrow of fortune is shot.
It strikes the target
Or buries its tip in the ground.
Since I've met my new lover
My heart flies after her all on its own.

13

By drawing diagrams on the ground
The stars of space can be measured.
Though familiar with the soft flesh
Of my lover's body
I cannot measure her depths.

14

I tied a prayer flag for my new beloved
At the side of a willow tree.
Keeper of willows,
Please don't tear it down.

15

So taken by her
I asked, "Will you be my companion?"
She said, "Only death can part us.
In this life nothing will."

16

This moon fades away.
Next month's moon will shine again.
My lover and I shall meet
When the lucky full moon rises.

17

Thinking of my long-time lover—
Does she lack shame and faithfulness?
Too bad her turquoise head-dress
Can't talk!

Songs of Doubt

18

Your smile with white teeth flashing
Is meant to lead this young man on—
But if you really want me
Please, lady, swear it from the depths of your
   heart.

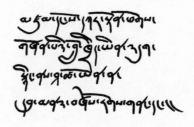

19

You come dressed in pure white
Like the three-day crescent moon—
But when you pledge yourself to me
Swear an oath full as the mid-month moon.

20

Is this girl not born from her mother
But from an apricot tree?
New love fades
Quick as apricot blossoms.

21

Lover, sincere one,
Soft flesh within this bed—
Are you not deceitful
To steal this young man's wealth and virtue?

22

Any dog—a tiger dog, a leopard dog—
Becomes tame when given food.
But this long-haired tigress of the tavern
Becomes more vicious when tamed.

Songs of Loss

23

Girl, lover for a short while,
Isn't she kin to the wolf?
Even given heaps of meat and skin
She bolts and runs for the mountains.

24

Lover who was joy to me,
Married to another—
This sickness of mind
Though inside
Consumes the flesh of the body.

25

Beloved lost to that thief—
It's time to throw a Mo.
That girl—was she sincere?—
Still haunts my dreams.

26

Though the ferry has no mind,
Its carved horse head turns to look at me.
But my faithless lover
Didn't even glance back.

27

Mind-stealing goddess,
I am the hunter who caught you.
But the powerful ruler Norsang Gyelbu
Stole you from me.

28

When I held the jewel in hand
I didn't know its worth.
When I lost it to another
The wind of loss howled in my chest.

29

Small black written letters
Can be destroyed by water or crossed out.
An unscribed figure in the mind may fade
But will never be forgotten.

30

Tonight's moon appears
Like the full moon of mid-month.
But the rabbit in the moon
Is fading, as if his time has ended.

31

Sumeru
Ri Rab Mountain
Stands at the center of the world
Steady and unchanging.
Just so, I doubt the sun and moon
Will move from their proper orbits.

32

Wild horses running in the hills
Can be caught with snares or lassos
But not even magic charms can stop
A lover's heart that's turned away.

Songs of Experience

33

A flower withers in a month's time.
But the turquoise bee doesn't grieve.
At the ending of an affair
I will not grieve either.

34

I and a girl of the marketplace
Tied a love-knot with three words.
I didn't undo it with my little ivory awl—
It just fell apart of its own accord.

35

Lovers who met while traveling
Were fixed up by the wine-shop woman.
If trouble or debts are born from this,
Please take care of her for me.

36

First, best not to see.
Then mind won't be captivated.
Next, best not to become intimate.
Then mind won't be trapped.

37

The dragon-demon's thorns
Should be neither feared nor ignored.
Without hesitation
I'll pick the sweet sugar apple in front.

38

A cloud yellow outside, black inside
Is a source of frost and hail.
A man who wears neither layman's black nor
    monk's yellow
Is an enemy of the Buddha's teachings.

Songs of Impermanence

39

Last year the grass was green and young.
This year clumps of dry straw wave.
By age a young man's body
More than a southern bow is bent.

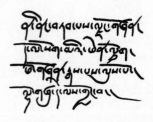

40

Face of frost on grass,
Icy north wind's messenger—
Robber of the bond
Between the bee and the flower.

41

Enchanted with the marsh
The geese want to stay a while
But their minds are already resigned
To the ice freezing over water.

42

If young girls never died
There would be no need to brew beer.
At such a time
This is a young man's surest source of refuge.

43

If a man doesn't ponder death and
    impermanence
Deep in his heart
He may both be clever and learned
But is like an idiot
Concerning the purpose of life.

44

Having lost my mind to her—
My sleep breaks in the night,
In the day she is not at hand.
What good to rack my mind so?

Songs of Secrecy

45

Earth frozen on top, soft beneath,
Is no place to lead a stallion.
Do not tell your deepest secrets
To your secret lovers.

46

Secrets not told to parents
But told to a casual lover,
Are told to her many stags
And heard by all his enemies.

47

A letter closed with a seal
Doesn't know how to speak.
Stamp a seal of discretion and care
On the mind of each of us.

48

You, bird, talkative parrot
Please keep your mouth shut.
I want to hear the sweet song
Of Elder Sister Thrush
In the willows.

49

The meeting place for me and my love
Is the dense forest of the southern valley.
Except for the chattering parrot
No one knows about it.
Please, talkative parrot
Don't give away our secret.

50

The willow's in love with the sparrow,
The sparrow's in love with the willow.
With love so intermingled
What chance does the gray hawk have?

51

People talk about me.
What they say may be true.
But just three short steps
Take me to the wine house of my lover.

52

Wind and rocks
Have battered the eagle's feathers.
I too have been torn apart
By deceivers and liars.

53

Don't tell me,
"Tsangyang! you're depraved."
Just like you
I desire pleasure and comfort, too.

Songs of Discovery

54

The old dog barks,
Senses sharper than any man's.
Do not announce
"He goes out!" at dusk
"He comes back!" at dawn.

55

I sought my lover at twilight
Snow fell at daybreak.
Residing at the Potala
I am Rigdzin Tsangyang Gyatso
But in the back alleys of Shol-town
I am rake and stud.
Secret or not
No matter.
Footprints have been left in the snow.

Songs of Retreat

56

Continually I think,
If come to holy Dharma,
In this same life,
In this same body,
A Buddha I could be.

57

Doing what my lover wishes
I lose my chance for Dharma.
But wandering in lonely mountain retreats
Opposes my lover's wishes.

58

If the girl who has stolen my heart
Leaves and turns to holy Dharma,
I, the young man, will also leave
And go wandering to mountain retreats.

59

Face to face with a venerable lama
Having come to ask for spiritual guidance
My mind won't stay—
It slips away toward my lover.

60

Meditating, my lama's face
Does not shine in mind.
Unbidden my lover's face
Again and again appears.

61

Holy oracle Lama Dorje
Who abides in the state
Just before Buddhahood—
If you have the power and ability
Liberate even the enemies of Dharma.

Tantric Songs

62

Pure glacial waters from Crystal Peak
And dewdrops from a vajra-plant,
Fermented with the yeast of ambrosia,
Brewed by the dakini of wisdom.
If drunk with pure commitment
The misery of lower states
Need never be experienced.

63

Not one night without a lover have I slept.
Nor one drop of the precious bodhi-seed have
   I spent.

Songs of Departure

64

He put his hat on his head.
Tossed his hair over his shoulder.
"Go in peace."
"Stay in peace."
"Will you be sad?"
"We'll meet again soon?"

ཕུ་ཆུ་ཁུ་ལའ་ཅ་ཞིག་པ།།
ཕུ་རྒྱུ་རྗེག་ལའ་ཕུག་པ།།
ག་ལའ་ཆོ་ཞག་ཉག་གུ་ཡུ་ཞེ།
ག་ལའ་ཅ་ཕ་ནག་ཉིག་ཅུ་ཞེ།
ཉག་པ་ཕལ་པ་སྒྱ་ལ་ཡ་ཕུ་ཞེ།
འཆག་པ་ར་ཕུ་རུ་ཅུ་གྱུ་ཡུ་གུ།།

65

I have asked so much
Of you
In this short life.
May we meet again
In the childhood of the next.

Song of Death

66

Yama, mirror of karma,
Ruler of the realm of death.
In this life things didn't go right.
May they go better in the next.

Song of Rebirth

67

That bird—white crane
Lend me your skill of wing.
I will not go far
I'll return near Litang.

Notes

INTRODUCTION

1. Kalsung Dhondup, *The Water-Horse and Other Years: A History of Seventeen- and Eighteenth Century Tibet* (Dharamsala: Library of Tibetan Works and Archives, 1984), pp. 51–52.

2. Michael Aris, *Hidden Treasures and Secret Lives: A Study of Pemalingapa* (London: Kegan Paul International, 1989), p. 144.

3. Zahiruddin Ahmad, *Sino-Tibetan Relations in the Seventeenth Century.* Serie Orientale Roma 40 (Roma: Instituts Italiano Per Il Medio Ed Estremo Oriente, 1970), p. 42.

4. Aris, *Hidden Treasures*, p. 159.

5. Helmet Hoffman, "Historical Introduction," in *Wings of the White Crane: Poems of Tshangs dbyangs rgya mtsho,* trans. by G. W. Houston (New Delhi: Motilal Banarsidass, 1982), p. xvii.

6. Aris, *Hidden Treasures*, p. 164.

7. Aris, *Hidden Treasures*, p. 165.

8. Aris, *Hidden Treasures*, p. 166.

9. Ahmad, *Sino-Tibetan Relations in the Seventeenth Century,* p. 332.

10. Sir Charles Bell, *Portrait of the Dalai Lama* (London: Collins Publishers, 1946), p. 36.

11. Rolf A. Stein, *Tibetan Civilization,* trans. J. E. Stapleton Driver (Stanford, CA: Stanford Univ. Press, 1972), p. 153.

POEMS

1. Ma-skyes-a-ma, our "face not born of mother," is literally "not born mother." It has been translated as

"young girl," or "virginal maiden." Mark Tatz suggests that it may refer to the Sixth Dalai Lama's step-mother, or to the young girl born of an apricot tree in a later poem. However, 'face' is honorific here, and is used as a metaphor for the "true nature of mind," (the "original face" of Zen), which is often described as unborn and compared to a luminous full moon.

3. Kongpo is a country district. The "young kid" may be another incarnation-in-training.

4. Chung Gyal was the birthplace of the Fifth Dalai Lama. According to one story, the Sixth Dalai Lama was destined to have a son with a girl from Chung Gyal, thus making the office of the Dalai Lama hereditary. However, due to the "lack of virtuous merit" in Tibet at the time, he was unable to meet the girl from Chung Gyal.

5. The wind-horse, symbol of good luck and primordial confidence, is a popular image on prayer-flags.

6. As the flower offers herself to the temple, the turquoise bee asks her to take him. Marion Duncan suggests: "This may be a double figure here as temples house both gods and goddesses; and he is led to her like the bee going into the goddess house to visit the flowers. This quatrain probably has a concealed sex meaning."

The "turquoise bee" is the Sixth Dalai Lama's poetic nom de plume.

8. ". . . in the depths of the sea" may be a pun on Gyatso or "ocean" in Tsangyang Gyatso's name.

9. White turquoise is more common and less valued than green or blue.

11. Mon, the southern border district and birthplace of the Sixth Dalai Lama, is now in Berkhar, Arunachal Pradesh, India.

12. The arrow may be a "lot-arrow," which tells a fortune depending on where it lands.

16. The full moon falls on mid-month. It is a day set aside for spiritual observances such as confession, fasting, and meditation.

20. "Girl not born from her mother" may refer to the first poem.

22. Tiger and leopard dogs are types of Tibetan dogs.

25. "Throw a Mo" refers to a method of divination sometimes performed by a lama throwing dice or using the beads of a rosary.

26. Tibetan ferries had wooden figureheads in the shape of a horse's head. Here, either the figurehead is turned back or the poet imagines it to be so.

27. According to Tatz, Norsang Gyelbu refers to an Indian king, whose hunter captured a female spirit, which the king then appropriated.

30. In Tibet, China, and Japan, "the rabbit in the moon...," like our "man in the moon," is a figure seen in the full moon.

31. Ri Rab Mountain (Sumeru), the central mountain, or axis mundi is Mt. Kailas. The sun and moon may refer to the Sixth Dalai Lama and his lover.

34. "Little ivory." An implement something like a large toothpick used to untie knots, and carried by any well-dressed Tibetan.

37. "Dragon-demon's thorns" may refer to other people's opinions or to his lover's parents or husband.

38. This poem may well be taken as a personal reflection on giving up his monk's roles.

39. A "southern bow" refers to the bamboo bows imported from the south.

42. Refuge refers ironically to the Buddhist custom of taking refuge in the Buddha.

46. The phrase "are told to her many stags" refers to his consort's other lovers.

53. This poem refers to the Desi, or regent, who, despite his own taste for women and wine, tried to convince Tsangyang Gyatso to act like a monk. The poem appears in the introduction to K. Dhondup's book, in a slightly different version, as "attributed to the Sixth Dalai Lama," but is not given in the text of his compilation of the poems.

54. Some take the "old dog" to be a meddling monk.

56. Tantric or Vajrayana Buddhism teaches that practitioners can obtain liberation in one lifetime.

60. Meditating on the lama's face is a form of guru-yoga.

62. This is a pure tantric song, which can possibly be understood to reconcile the conflicting spiritual/romantic poles of Tsangyang Gyatso's life. The Tibetan *dakini*, which translates as "sky-goer," is a tantric deity or goddess who may manifest as a human consort. "Pure commitment" is *samaya*, a tantric religious vow. "Vajra" is "diamond" or "adamantine," as in Vajrayana or Diamond Vehicle, also known as Tantra. According to John A. Ardussi, in "Brewing and Drinking the Beer of Enlightenment in Tibetan Buddhism": "Beer or alcoholic drink as a symbol for nectarous essence (*amrita*; in Tibetan, *bdud-rtsi*)—the refined essential of teachings or contemplative experiences—is common in Tibetan Buddhist writing and initially derives from Indian usage. . . . Both the preparation and the drinking serve as symbols of yogic endeavor."

63. Tatz does not include this song. Dhondup, however, includes it in the introduction to his translation as an example of verses that "indirectly show his deep knowledge of and practice of tantra." Dhondup's translation reads:

> *Never have I slept without a sweetheart*
> *Nor have I spent a single drop of sperm.*

Dhondup adds, "This claim of control over his flow of sperm openly declares his profound grasp and mastery of tantric practices."

Yu also leaves it out of his translation, but he too mentions it in his introduction. "A Tibetan told me that in one of his biographical works there is a verse saying, 'Without a girl, he never slept, be that as it may, he never defiled his chastity,' and many Tibetans believed in it." In his note to this passage, Yu gives us the transliterated version: "In Tibetan: *gong re nang mo med pa nyal ma myong/ thig le gnyung dkar tsam zhig gtong ma myong*," and comments, "It is rather indecent if translated literally, and I think it is not from his biography."

The key word here is *thig le*, which is a Tibetan translation of the Sanskrit *bindu*, or seed. The word may refer to sperm or/and be taken in a more symbolic metaphysical sense. In the secret or esoteric yogic tradition of Buddhist Tantra, *thig le* is associated with bodhicitta, "the mind of enlightenment," hence our translation as "precious bodhi-seed."

66. Yama, the god or deity of death, holds a mirror that reflects one's deeds or actions (*karma*).

67. Litang is a town in eastern Tibet. This poem was taken as a prophecy of the place of rebirth of the next (Seventh) Dalai Lama, who was indeed recognized there.

Bibliography

TRANSLATIONS

Barks, Coleman. *Stallion on a Frozen Lake.* Athens, Ga: Maypop, 1993.

Dhondup, Kalsang. *Songs of the Sixth Dalai Lama.* Dharamsala: Library of Tibetan Works and Archives, 1981.

Duncan, Marion H. *Love Songs and Proverbs of Tibet.* London: Mitre Press, 1961, pp. 119–35.

Houston, G. W. *Wings of the White Crane: Poems of Tshangs dbyangs rgya mtsho.* Delhi: Motilal Banarsidass, 1982.

Tatz, Mark. "Songs of the Sixth Dalai Lama." *The Tibet Journal,* 4 (1981), pp. 13–31.

Yu Dawchuyuan. *Love Songs of the Sixth Dalai Lama.* Peiking: Academica Sinica Monograph Series, A, no. 5, 1930.

SECONDARY SOURCES

Ahmad, Zahiruddin. *Sino-Tibetan Relations in the Seventeenth Century.* Serie Orientale Roma 40. Roma: Insituto Italiano Per Il Medio Ed Estremo Oriente, 1970.

Ardussi, John A. "Brewing and Drinking the Beer of Enlightenment in Tibetan Buddhism: The Doha Tradition in Tibet." *Journal of the American Oriental Society* 97.2 (1977); 115–24.

Aris, Michael. *Hidden Treasures and Secret Lives: A Study of Pemalingapa (1450–1521) and the Sixth Dalai (1683–1706).* London: Kegan Paul International, 1989.

Bell, Sir Charles. *Portrait of the Dalai Lama*. London: Collins Publishers, 1946.

Dhondup, Kalsang. *The Water-Horse and Other Years: A History of Seventeen- and Eighteenth-Century Tibet*. Dharamsala: Library of Tibetan Works and Archives, 1984.

Dowman, Keith, and Paljor, Sonam., trans. *The Divine Madman: The Sublime Life and Songs of Drukpa Kunley*. London: Routledge and Kegan Paul, 1980.

Karmay, Samten Gyaltsen. *Secret Visions of the Fifth Dalai Lama: The Gold Manuscripts in the Fournier Collection*. London: Serindia Publications, 1988.

Kemp, Richard. *The Potala of Tibet*. London: Stacey International, 1988.

Norbu, Thubten Jigme, and Turnbull, Colin. *Tibet*. New York: Simon & Schuster, 1968.

Petech, Luciano C. *China and Tibet in the Early Eighteenth Century*. Leiden: E. J. Brill, 1950.

Richardson, Hugh. *Tibet and Its History*. Boston: Shambhala Publications, 1984.

Shakabpa, Tsepan. *Tibet: A Political History*. New Haven, CT: Yale Univ. Press, 1967.

Snellgrove, David, and Richardson, Hugh. *A Cultural History of Tibet*. New York: Praeger Publishers, 1968.

Stein, Rölf A. *Tibetan Civilization*. Translated by J. E. Stapleton Driver. Stanford, CA: Stanford Univ. Press, 1972.

Acknowledgments

Both Rick Fields and Brian Cutillo would like to acknowledge the quiet inspiration of Arthur Mandlebaum, devoted lotsawa-translator, steady practitioner, and dedicated teacher of the Tibetan language.